to burn by fire light

MJ Bachman

Presentation by *BookLeaf Publishing*

Web: www.bookleafpub.com

E-mail: info@bookleafpub.com

ISBN: 9789357616911

First edition 2022

to mom, who has always read the first draft.

and to dad, who encouraged me to do it.

ACKNOWLEDGEMENT

The journey to writing this collection of poems would have been so different had it not been for the amazing writing faculty at Murray State University. Thank you for believing in me.

PREFACE

Dear reader,

This is a look into my brain. It's not revolutionary, but I hope maybe it might mean something to you, even if it's just a quick read.

With love,

       mj

gas leak

she went from a burning home,
to one that was silently, lethally,
filling with gas.
tasteless, odorless, and
invisible.
the repercussions of ignoring the
lightheadedness and irritability
and words that slit scars into the
soft flesh of her mutilated heart were
stinging, boiling, and
infected.
tiny flames licking at the
gaping wounds of desire.
she hadn't wanted this for herself:
trained into believing she was at fault, a soloist,
an expert
in emotional damage control.
delicate and ritualistically cautious
of the eggshell-landmines,
she was award-winning in de-escalation.
toes pointed, shoulders back, and
noiselessly
she lands in the crevices,
the walls of superiority
providing a blind spot of negligence.

bending, contorting, and
chipping away at herself,
in hopes she will be called a masterpiece.

the gas makes her delusional
after years of exposure,
and she Allows herself to fantasize about
the ashes of the burning house.
smoke billows out,
serpents of sparks hissing, gnashing, and
she wonders if the first responders
will make it in time.

her chest is collapsing in and
the smoke is scorching her throat.
there are no reparations for what has been
inflicted.
she didn't light the match,
so why is she the only one burning?

she lets the smoke fill her lungs
willingly now,
the unseen assailant waging war
on her deteriorating organs.
there are so many things left Unsaid.
and the fire has burned itself from
a blazing, terrifying, and
overwhelming force of nature
to a burnt ember,

the glow barely visible in
the shimmering air.

she dies of inhalation and
no one is shocked. this rabbit-hole leads
here every time,
and this is the ending.

Rinse
and Repeat.

she's out of time.
she wishes, one last time, something
about trampling the land mines,
shattering them.
she wishes she could have blown up
with them, becoming a star,
never to burn out.

say that's what happened instead,
okay?

one.

she wonders if the door knows her
warmth like she knows its cool
embrace. knees drawn tight to her
chest with her quivering chin
nestled in the divot they create. the
Mirage of safety shimmered with
promise, whispering of change what
was certain to come.
certain.
the wood muffles the shouting and
the brown against the undusted
baseboards stands defiantly against the
eggshell walls.

two.

a kind woman with the blue uniform
and the yellow badge knelt in the
frame of the front door, fastening
the straps of the devastatingly small
shoes. soothing words couldn't erase
the diamond tears that stained
pale cheeks.
the girl could take flight at any moment,
even if her broken wings
would only carry her away from there.

her hand was tiny in the woman's,
red and blue lights taking to court
the monsters under her bed
who are legally stripped from their titles,

forcing the baby bird to jump from
a burning nest.

family ties

            blood   is thicker
than   water
                        of the covenant
the   of the

womb.
I say to my reflection,
            but my eyes are not my own,
                        mixed with the blue from the
Bird.
my hair existed before it
            was on my head
                                    from the Bee.
from nest   to   hive,
                        the water
of the womb has dried
                        u p
and I am left

            with honey

            and   sticks

covered in blood.

the branches of my family tree grow from
            scattered roots.
                        Are you angry
or proud that   I'm preventing
root

                                        rot?

natural predator

your words are like vipers,
hissing and whispering praise
when i do right by you.
my success will
indoctrinate me into time.
you constrict against my white wings
like a natural predator.
am i bound to be no more than i am now, or
do i have time to change and experience
flight?
the trees yawn upwards, and in the leaves-
change.

i think
i want
I wish you will emerge,
flourishing the changes that no longer erode
my wings, plucking my feathers until
i am flightless.
when you emerge, will you tenderly
send me off?
or will i fall from the nest and
learn the severity of fight
or flight?

i think
i wish
I know the answer will not change
because your nest blew from the tree
and landed among leaves—
trampled underfoot of animals who
scamper onwards,

I will learn to fly.

three.

she was too young to have privacy-
her aunt said. what if she gets hurt
and the door is closed? the scratchy
beach towel with an
outdated cartoon character's smile
drawn on was hung in its place
because she wouldn't sleep if the
light from the hallway could infect
the bedroom.

how tragic.

four.

the yellow bus stopped at the end of
the street framed by green stalks
of growing corn, and she emerged, a
pink jacket to match her Dora
backpack. did the bus driver see the
car that waited for her?

it was around the corner before she
noticed the man emerge from the
car.
   the Bee.
with her hair
 and her eyes.
she had never been so grateful for
the lashes that the corn left on her cheeks as she
was as
she ran like a feral cat,
darting away from
     what was
    and
     what could become
with only the familiar shouting and a flash of
silver she had seen to haunt her as she arrived at
the front door to the
house she occupied,
twenty minutes late and sobbing hysterically.

summer

the linen dries in
the hot summer breeze,
    and her hair carries itself,
curls   separated
by the fine fingers of
             the   wind.
her skin is freckled by
             the   sun,
the time that passes as she reads,
the rays that filter through clouds
       leaving lasting impressions.

the breeze smells like
suburbia   and freshly   mown lawns.
      she tends to the kids and the garden.

she is a mother,
   & a wife, & a daughter
     she is chicken noodle soup when sick &
    a lavender-scented pillow when tired.
    she is warm meals & a tight hug
her shoulders heavy   with tears,
but her smiles never
cracks.

the kids will go back to school in the fall,
        with their bulletproof backpacks
and 9-1-1 saved into their phones.
                        and she will crave the
noise
                    that drives her to escape
to the yard,
                            doing
laundry.
        she is riddled with fears,
            but she smiles because
she is a mother, &
  a daughter & a wife

and it is summer.

remnants

you've changed.

neither positive nor negative,
simply an observation of the obvious.

behind you, i see the remnants
of who you once were, the life you once led.

guided by invisible wires,
who is the puppeteer?

you?
no.

the displayed remnants have fallen from the nest
and
you are changed

not on your own accord,
but because you had to.

i still love you,
i whisper to my reflection.

she smiles.

five.

15

the visitation room was quiet,
except for the beads that hung in the frame
for a door.
she hated the noise.
  click,   clack,
        click,
  clack,   click.
she just wanted to watch
Punky Brewster.

six.

it's new.

it lasts six months.

they get pregnant and her clothes
are in a trash bag on the wrong side
of the door.

A Benediction of Change

i'm   sorry
          the word tumbles out of my mouth
when i
                    brush someone's shoulder
                                             or
cough a little too loud

          for a little too long
i'm   sorry
                                             it is
rushed
and usually   very

          v e r y
quiet.
i'm   sorry
                                        loses its
meaning when it is
tossed out
like pocket   change,
                                             i

apologize on
a drop
of a dime,
for things

out   of   my
control.

it is love,

the kind that holds up a mirror when
i beg for redemption
                                        and
assures me there is no need

                                        to

apologize.

it is then
                              i'm
sorry
                                        i'm
        sorry
                        i'm
sorry

becomes
                                        thank
        you
                              thank
you
                    thank   you
thank
                you

                                    for
reminding me that

        my riches are   sacred
thank
        you

for blessing me

                                in compassion
that I have
blindly robbed
            myself of.
thank
        you.

to my past self:

my Dear,

the world you have created in your perception
is filled with
mold and the remains of bone marrow.
dust away the dirt and grime you have
long since grown too accustomed
and view the world.

leave the rose-colored glasses to their solitude
and see the world as it is:
        it is love
                & heartbreak.
        it is family
                & grief.
        it is adventure
                & trauma.
do not let the darkness of it all
extinguish your light. find fuel in what is
        right
                & just
        & thoughtful
                & well-intentioned.

keep going,
        my dear

seven.

it's newer, and she mistakes the
garage for the front door.

she doesn't know better. she wears
face paint of kitten whiskers when
she meets her grandparents for the first time.

house codes
        &neighborhood disputes,
she understands the
rhythm of life here and its
permanence.

she likes it.

eight.

the new neighbors are nice. she
doesn't talk to them, but her
parents are happier. things are
happier.

the garage door has a camera, and
she waves to it before
she leaves.

nine.

she's so grown up. comments from
relatives as she moved into her
college dorm. she was grown up. but

she stills misses the nest and finds comfort
in the little notes, sticks of advice,
tucked in her bag.

she hangs a tapestry over the door and sets her
teddy
bear among the sticks.

molting

why do the leaves keep changing?

as a hatchling,
i was more of an adult
than i am now,
on the brink of
21.

no time for pleasantries,
like sitting on telephone-lines or
hanging upside-down on the monkey bars.
my feathers have scattered to the wind
i find myself looking to it
for solace,
full of wisdom and change.
i was mature,
an old soul.

oh,
how i want to
cradle her in the palm of her hand
and brush my thumb over
her beak
and tell her
how proud i am
that we have made it
this far.

a snail's pace

I remember the way the wind tickled my
exposed skin
as you wrapped your arms around me.
Your birdsong of sweet nothingness into my
listening ear. I would listen to your song for
days, and I did.

Sun-filled days with an absence of clouds melted
into
moonless nights broken up with rainstorms and
my arms around you. I remember how you
would comfort my shaking shoulders and your
warm breath against my cheek
as we talk in the darkness. We were so excited
for the future-
so enraptured by the idea that
we soared stateside,
without looking at the signs we were passing.
I didn't care.
Neither did you.
But now, I feel like something has grounded me,
rooting my feet into the soil.
For the first time, I don't panic.
I don't run.
I can't. I look at where we are.

In the moment, surrounded by personal
responsibilities and drowning in assignments
and… you.
Your face shines, not as bright as it once was, a
five o'clock shadow tracing the jaw and
cheekbones of your soft face.
Your eyes don't glitter- they burn with
excitement and the golden ring that encircles
your pupil seems to swirl within your eyes. In
frozen moments, everything is so loud: love that
keeps pulsing from you and pulling me back in.
Anger, exhaustion, passion, hunger.
All present, all overwhelming.
At our breakneck rush forward, we hadn't
noticed them.
The feeling is everything I needed.
Maybe we could live in now as we move at a
snail's pace.
I'd like that.

ten.

it's a three bed, two bath, and he
carries her over the threshold of the
door like she is a bird, and he is her
nest.

she sleeps away from the door, and
he pulls the covers up.

napkin confession

the red in you cheeks
                    like petals from a fallen
rose
burns in the cold-
                    the wind whipping,
hair twisting and dancing.

is it a love poem when these thoughts
                          are no longer

romanticized?
when talking all night
                    becomes comforting
silence,
and bundles of roses,
                    becomes bringing home
groceries,

we're still in love,

right?
is it a love poem when it becomes about
us,   subconsciously,
  and no longer me and you,
                    separately?

                        do our identities melt
together?

do you want them to?

is it still a love poem,
                    it it is not about
                                    falling
                                        in
love,
        but what we haven't seen-
                            if it is about
staying in
love?

the C-word

the word has power,
the way it drips from the doctor's lips
like poisoned honey
dripping from an IV and
my mother
& my grandmother
recoil.

we talk about it,
separately,
upon hushed whispers &
concerned murmurs that
leave lasting imprints
on my heart and when the
room goes dark and
the birds stop singing,
i cry alone.
because it is
my mother
& my grandmother.

the foundation of femininity:
the brush of lipstick after dinner,
the way i toss my hair,
the way i hold my knee's together to keep

an imaginary dime from
dropping between them.
these were lessons taught from
honey-suckle, feminine foundations of
generations.

we don't talk about the C-word.
we don't talk about the fabric of femininity
that are cut from
my mother
& my grandmother.

breast,
ovaries,
femininity.

haircuts,
button-down shirts,
radiation.

my boyfriend knows
the C-word
and the power it wields
when it leaves
clumps of hair in the shower
after his mother gets
ready for work.

my best friends know the power of

the C-word
when we remind each other
to check for lumps
with the right form, so you don't
miss a lymph-node
(because it's so much worse if it gets into the
lymph-nodes)
And we giggle, in silent relief,
when we are clear.

the woman in my life are haunted by
the C-word.
the word spread its tendrils of terror
until it is crushing my heart.
    i am afraid.
    & my mother is afraid.
    & my grandmother is afraid.
    & my boyfriend's mother is afraid.
    & my best friend is afraid.
and there is no happy ending
no conclusion
because it does not end
with my mother
and my grandmother-

the C-word
knows no language barrier.
knows no color.
knows no gender.

the C-word
is ruthless
and anger
and decay.
the C-word
is my worst enemy and
it does not know me like
i know its hideous reality.

but the women in my life
show me their femininity
in their love
and in their courage
and even when
the C-word
comes back to revoke
it all,
my mother
& my grandmother
& the other women in my life who know
the C-word
like a bad friend:

stay strong.
stay feminine.
stay loved
because it is something
cancer
cannot revoke.